Backyard Science

Chris Maynard

A PEARSON COMPANY

LONDON, NEW YORK, SYDNEY, DELHI, PARIS, MUNICH, and JOHANNESBURG

Project Editor   Penelope York
Art Editor   Jacqueline Gooden
Publishing Manager   Mary Ling
Managing Art Editor   Rachael Foster
Photography   Steve Shott
Jacket Design   Chris Drew
DTP Designer   Almudena Díaz
Picture Research   Marie Osborn
Production   Kate Oliver

Science Educational Consultant
Alison Porter

The scientists
Emily Couchman, Ashley Mclarty, Amy Wiggins

First American Edition, 2001

00 01 02 03 04 05 10 9 8 7 6 5 4 3 2 1

Published in the United States by
DK Publishing, Inc.
95 Madison Avenue
New York, New York 10016

Copyright © 2001 Dorling Kindersley Limited

Library of Congress Cataloging-in-Publication Data

Backyard Science.-- 1st American ed.
    p. cm.
Includes index.
ISBN 0-7894-6971-5
  1. Science--Experiments--Juvenile literature. [1. Science--Experiments. 2.
Experiments. 3. Science projects.] 1. Dorling Kindersley Publishing, Inc.

Q164.B25 2001
507'.8--dc21

00-057049

All rights reserved under International and Pan-American Copyright Conventions.
No part of this publication may be reproduced, stored in a retrieval system, or
transmitted in any form or by any means, electronic, mechanical, photocopying,
recording, or otherwise, without the prior written permission of the copyright
owner. Published in Great Britain by Dorling Kindersley Limited.

ISBN 0-7894-6971-5

Color reproduction by Colourscan, Singapore
Printed and bound in Italy by L.E.G.O.

See our complete
catalog at
dk.com

Contents

Backyard Lab

HOW CAN AN ORDINARY BACKYARD be good for science? After all, there's not much in it. Or is there? Come to think of it, backyards are really labs of life. Even in a small plot you can spend days doing biology, zoology, meteorology, and much, much more – it's "ology" city out there! So arm yourself with the right equipment, get out, and discover your own backyard.

Whenever you pick up a bug to study it, be sure to return it to the yard unharmed.

Some scientists are very neat – others are olympic-class slobs.

When science goes well you can really get a lift out of it.

How to study backyard science

Backyard science can take a lot of patience. But it is great fun. As you do the experiments, read the science stuff in the boxes.

The science stuff

These colored boxes and panels are there to explain the science part. Read them as you are doing the experiments so that you understand why you are doing them.

These bugs are amazing!

Not all experiments go according to plan; that's science for you!

Time for some fun.

What's happening over there? Did you say "do a worm dance?"

Wherever you see this sign, ask an adult to help you.

If you see this sign, be sure to be extra careful.

This sign is to remind you to treat animals with respect and to return them carefully to where they came from when you have finished studying them.

Keeping a science logbook is important. Write down all the things you find or sketch them – you may need to label drawings so that people can understand your pictures. Use cameras, charts, and collect samples as well. Finally, sit back and admire the record of everything you've learned.

Survival Special

WHAT DO YOU NEED TO SURVIVE? A warm home, lots of food, and a bed? Well a plant needs its comforts too. Find out what it needs and what happens if it doesn't get exactly what it wants.

Fruit cocktail

How often do you open your lunch box, eat the fruit inside it, and then throw the seeds or pits away? Next time hang on to them and try growing your own plants. Observe the whole amazing process from seed to sandwich.

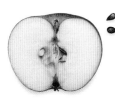

Tomato seeds   Orange seeds   Apple seeds   Avocado pit

Choose your favorite fruit; tomatoes are good for this experiment since they are quick and easy to grow. Plant three pots of tomato seeds about 0.2 in (0.5 cm) below the surface of some rich compost. Water them enough so that the soil is damp – not soaking. Make some labels to stick in the pots so that you can tell them apart.

Seeds don't need light to start growing because all the food they require is stored inside them.

Put the pots into zip-top bags, which act like mini greenhouses, and stick them in a warm, dark place. After 2-3 weeks, the shoots will appear. Take them out of their bags, give them light, and water them regularly. You will use these three plants for your next experiment.

The coco-de-mer seed, the biggest seed in the world, is as big as a chicken

Leave one plant in the light but deny it water.

Give one tomato plant lots of water and light.

Put a bucket over one of them but water it regularly.

Plant science

Sun

CO²

Nutrients

H_2O

To survive, plants trap sunlight, breathe air (which has got carbon dioxide – CO_2 – gas in it), and drink water (H_2O). They need minerals too – just like humans need vitamins – that their roots absorb from the soil. A chemical reaction takes place in the leaves as all these ingredients are pulled together. The reaction is called photosynthesis, and this makes the food that a plant needs in order to grow.

Deny them if you dare

When your plants have grown it is time to find out what happens if they don't have water or light. You will need to deny one plant water, one light, and give the last one both, as above. Watch what happens every day. One will grow to be healthy. What happens to the other two? How quickly do they wilt, and which one wilts first? Record your results.

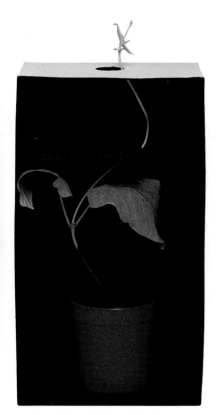

Most people think
that the tomato is a
vegetable but it is
actually a fruit

Exception?

Can any plants survive without water? Not for long. Even cacti need some water. They keep going by storing it in their fleshy stems.

Let there be light

Plants left in the dark will starve to death. No wonder they have a knack for finding light. Place a small plant in a shoe box with a hole at the top and two pieces of cardboard on the sides to hide the light. Put on the lid and open the box once a day to see the progress. The plant will writhe until it finds the light.

Root Power

WITHOUT ROOTS PLANTS WOULD be in lots of trouble. Plants feed themselves through roots and if they didn't have any they would fall over. Now you can prove what roots really do.

Back to the roots

Plants send their roots out under the ground to search for the water and nutrients that they need to grow. To take a look at some all-important root strands get a plant in a pot, moisten the soil, and remove it gently.

Growing up
Some stems have roots that grow above ground. They keep plants upright in the wind. They're called buttress roots and some grow as high as 30 ft (9 m).

Be very careful when you take the plant out, you don't want to break any of the hair-thin roots.

Root science

Roots have enormous strength. As they hunt for food and water they push through soil and rock like butter. Test this power yourself. Plant some seeds in an eggshell filled with damp potting soil. Put it in an eggcup and water regularly as the plants grow. In a short time the roots will feel squashed and will start to look for more room. The walls of the shell won't hold them for a moment as they search for freedom.

Root lab

Here's a great way to watch the progress of a root and stem – it's like having a secret window. Roll up some damp blotting paper and put it in a jar. Soak a bean overnight and place it between the paper and the glass.

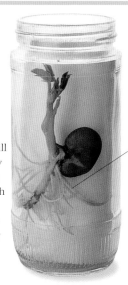

The roots will start to grow first, and no matter which way up the seed is, they always grow downward.

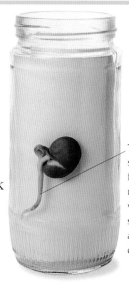

When the roots and stem are about this big, try turning the jar upside down. What do the roots do?

Drinking science

So plants can drink, but how? As water evaporates through tiny holes (stomata, see picture below) in the leaves and petals, fresh water is drawn up from below.

In a plant there is an unbroken tower of water running from the bottom to the top, and the force that draws water up the plant from the roots to the top is known as "transpiration."

Pink drink

The best way to drink a milkshake is through a straw. Plant roots drink in pretty much the same way – though they prefer plain water. Inside the plant there are bunches of thin tubes that carry water up the roots and stems and into the leaves. Try this colorful experiment to prove it.

Take some white flowers and put each one in a vase. Mix different food coloring and water in the vases. Leave them for several hours to see if their stems are like straws. Some flowers work better than others, so try different ones. How long does each one take to change color? How do you think the color got to the flowers?

Does the length or the thickness of the stem make a difference?

Do some colors work better than others?

Pull power

How powerful is transpiration? For starters, it can lift water all the way to the top of a 164 ft (50 m) chestnut tree without batting an eyelid.

A long story

Some plants have very long root networks. The hairy roots of rye plants – a type of grass – can stretch over 370 miles (600 km) if you lay them all end to end.

Roots grow downward because they obey the law of gravity

Floating Around

PEOPLE HAVE BEEN STEALING GOOD IDEAS from nature since the Stone Age. That's why parachutes and helicopters look suspiciously like some of the seeds that float across the backyard now and again.

Parachute copycat
A parachute works in the same way as the dandelion seed. The canopy opens, which makes the fall to the ground slower so that skydivers land softly – most of the time.

Get away seed

Why do seeds abandon their parents? Because big plants hog space, light, and water. Seeds must get as far away as possible to survive. Dandelion and thistle seeds have fluffy parachutes that trap the wind and waft them all over the place.

The seed is the weight at the bottom of the dandelion parachute.

The piece of modeling clay, like the seed, weighs the parachute down slightly to keep the canopy open.

Make your own parachute by cutting out a square piece of material. Tie a piece of string to each corner and attach the ends together around a piece of modeling clay, as shown. Let it fall from a height. The canopy opens, traps the air, and it falls slowly. If it is windy, how far does it travel before it hits the ground?

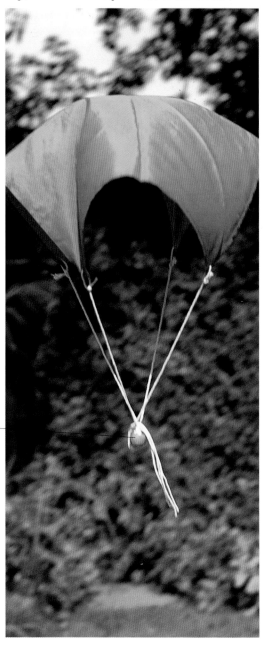

Copter copycat

Have you ever noticed maple seeds spinning around and around as they fall to the ground? They work like a helicopter – they have spinning wings that use air to fly. Try making your own helicopter wings.

In a spin

Make your own minicopter and see how far you can get it to spin away from you.

Copy this minicopter pattern onto a sheet of stiff paper – about as tall as a piece of 8 1/2 x 11 inch paper.

Cut along the solid lines and fold along the dotted lines. Fold the top flaps over in opposite directions.

Fold the bottom flap up and pin it with a paper clip. The added weight helps the minicopter to spin.

Watch as your minicopter floats through the air. The falling blades hit the air, forcing it outward with a sideways push. As the air flow shifts, the copter starts to spin. A maple seed shifts air in the same way except that the tip of the seed is bent slightly inward, which forces it to spin.

The balsam flower just needs an animal to brush against it, or a gust of wind to encourage it to send its seeds flying.

Dispersal science

Long before humans, flowering plants were busy figuring out ways to spread their seeds far and wide. They came up with three ways: animals, water, and the wind.

Birds and beasts

Animals and birds do an effective job of dispersal by having seeds cling to their fur or ride in their gut after they swallow them. Burrs hook themselves on to fur like velcro – in fact the idea for velcro came from burrs.

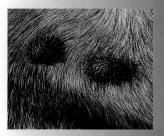

Seed passengers

Lotus plants grow in water and rely on the river to carry away their seeds. Poppies have pods like tiny pepperpots. They're full of seeds that are flung out when the wind rocks the plant. The balsam flower holds its seeds in little catapults. When jiggled, the seeds explode away.

Lotus plant

Opium poppy

Balsam flower

11

Birdwatch

BIRDS ARE HAPPY WHEN THE BACKYARD is full of tender worms and beetles. And if humans leave feeders for them – even better. Get them into your backyard with food they can't resist then study their behavior.

Bird chef

Bird food is nothing like the food we like to eat – but birds find it beak-smackingly good. It's packed with goodies to keep birds stocked up with the vitamins and fats that they need.

Take various kitchen scraps – oats, cooked rice, leftover vegetables, nuts, birdseed, bacon rind, or breadcrumbs – and mix them into a bowl. Ask an adult to pour some hot shortening into the bowl and mix until it is a gooey mess.

Fill a small flowerpot with the gooey mixture, stick a small twig through the middle of it, and put it in the fridge to set. When it is hard, ease out the set mixture. Tie some string around the stick and hang it on a branch.

You will need a large needle to thread the string through. But be careful not to prick yourself.

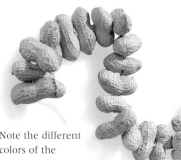

Note the different colors of the birds and identify them later.

Getting spotty

Three things will make you better at spotting birds – a pair of binoculars, a notebook, and lots of patience. How many different birds can you spot in a day, or in a week? Keep a log.

Take a handful of nuts and carefully thread them onto a piece of string. Peanuts work very well. The birds can easily crack open the nut necklace.

Warning! Don't put salty foods out for the birds. Their bodies can't take it.

Push the bird mixture tightly into a large pinecone and hang it up.

Try a mix of different nuts threaded onto a piece of string.

When you tie the food to the tree, make sure you tie the knots tightly – birds can be heavy.

A milk carton makes a fantastic birdseed holder for small birds. Simply cut a hole in one side, fill it with birdseed or nuts, and attach some string.

Bird food favorites

In winter birds can starve because it is so difficult to find food. There are very few bugs and seeds around. So you might be a lifesaver if you hang food out. Fatty foods, such as bacon rind and shortening, are particularly good for building body fat. Birds will appreciate food in warm weather too. So continue to hang food out and enjoy watching bird behavior all year.

Did you know?

Swifts spend almost their entire life flying. They only land to lay eggs and to look after their young.

Bird care

In addition to hanging feeders, fill a bowl of fresh water and put it nearby. The birds will enjoy splashing in it as they wash, as well as drinking it.

13

Feathered Friends

WHAT DOES A BACKYARD HOPPING with birds make you think of? Feathers? Eggs? Now imagine what a scientist thinks. Why do birds fly rather than nosedive downward? What is inside an egg?

What keeps them up?

Without feathers, a bird would be cold, wet, unable to fly, and extremely thin. Birds have down feathers, body feathers, tail, and wing feathers. What is each one for, and how do they work?

Flying science

If the feather is from a wingtip it has a curved surface. As a bird flies, air over the curved upper part flows faster than air that is passing below it. The difference in air speed above and below lifts up the whole feather. This lift keeps birds from crash landing.

How do flight feathers work?
Pin the shaft of a wing feather loosely to a stick, keeping the narrow edge facing you. Blow over the narrow edge of the feather and watch how it lifts. Now turn the feather around. What does it do this time?

Flight feathers are smooth and glossy. They are made from lightweight strands hooked tightly together.

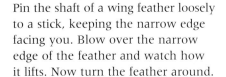

Body feathers are sometimes patterned at the top. This can be for camouflage or simply to show off.

Body feathers are downy and warm like a comforter. But they don't have much to do with flying. Some body feathers trap air to help insulation.

Tail feathers help birds to steer and balance as they fly.

Flight patterns

Birds fly in a lot of different ways. Study their flight patterns next time you are birdwatching and draw how they fly. A swift flys in all directions and swoops and soars. A finch flaps then glides for a while.

Swift flight

Finch flight

Egg science

It's unlikely that you'll see any fertilized eggs unless you go to a farm. Farmers use a metal can, very similar to your box, called a "candler" to tell if an egg is fertilized. If the yolk looks more solid then there is a chance a chick will grow.

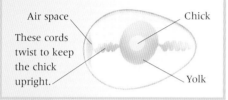

Air space

These cords twist to keep the chick upright.

Chick

Yolk

Eggs-ray eyes

How do you look inside a chicken egg without breaking it? Paint a shoe box black. Cut out a small hole in the lid. Place a flashlight in the box shining up through the hole. Go somewhere dark, turn on the flashlight, and put an egg over the hole. What do you see?

Hatching out

A mother bird sits on her eggs keeping them warm until they hatch. If you are lucky enough to see a nest in a tree, watch it from a distance. When the time comes for the chicks to hatch they have to work pretty hard to get out.

As the air in the end of the egg gets used up the chick pokes holes in the blunt end using the sharp tip of its beak.

It shoves hard with its feet to flip off the cap of the shell. When it breaks the chick starts to wriggle out.

The smallest egg of all is the bee hummingbird's. End to end it can be just 0.4 in long (1 cm) – about fingernail size.

The biggest egg in the world is an ostrich egg. You'd need to crack open at least a dozen chicken eggs to fill it up

Try making your own nest and imagine only using a beak and two feet.

Lichen and moss for camouflage.

Down feathers for insulation.

⚠ Nesting place

Never go near a bird's nest while it is full of eggs. If you touch the nest the mother bird will abandon it. Always watch from a distance. Take a look at the nest above. A bird uses many materials to make a safe, insulated home for its brood.

Within a few hours it runs around feeding itself. It does what takes us five years in a matter of a few hours.

Sound Effects

Ask an adult to tie the string securely to the shaft of wood.

STAND PERFECTLY STILL and listen hard. What can you hear? From the loudest clap of thunder to the scuttling of a mouse, our ears can identify sounds all around us like radar collecting information. But what makes the sound, and how do we come to hear them?

Make sure no one is standing near you when you swing.

Bull roarer

Here's a way to make the air vibrate so that it roars. Take a ruler-sized slat of wood and ask an adult to make a hole in one end. Tie a piece of string through the hole and swing it around your head at top speed. Can you feel the air vibrate as the wood roars?

Wave watch

Sound waves work like water waves – they'd look like them too if they were visible. Drop some water into a bowl and watch the waves spread out. Sound spreads just like this.

Sound science

Sound is a set of vibrations. They travel through the air in waves, just like water waves in a bowl. Your ears pick up these vibrations at your ear drum. The bull roarer vibrates the air as it spins and produces sound waves that "roar." You can also feel sound vibrations by touching your throat when you talk.

Sound game

Can you tell where a sound comes from? Not sure? Try this game. Blindfold one person and then place two or more friends around her. Take turns clapping, and the blindfolded person must point to where she thinks the sound comes from. It's not as easy as it sounds!

Take a big breath and blow the whistle for as long as you can.

Some jets can go faster than the speed of sound

High-low

A train hurtles into a station with a high-pitched roar that gets deeper the moment it thunders past you. Why? The answer is the Doppler Effect. Ask a friend to ride past fast, blowing a whistle. Fast-moving objects squeeze sound waves traveling in front of it, so they sound higher. Then they stretch them out behind, making them deeper.

Thunder clap

Sound is no slouch. But it is slow compared to the speed of light. That is why in a thunderstorm the lightning appears first, even though thunder booms and sends out its sound waves at exactly the same time. Sound travels 0.5 miles (0.3 km) in one second. During the next storm, count, in seconds, from when you see the lightning until you hear the thunder. You can then work out how far away the storm is.

Echo-o-o-o

An echo is a sound that has bumped headfirst into something and then bounced back. Bats use echoes to find their prey. As they fly in the dark they let out high-pitched squeaks that bounce off objects in front of them. Their ears pick up the faint echoes so they can work out where insects are flying in the dark.

17

⚠️🦋Bug Safari

THE FIRST THING PEOPLE NOTICE about bugs is this – boy there are a lot of them. We suspect there are zillions, although nobody can count that high. And what's their secret? It's that they can eat anything and live anywhere. Check it out in your backyard.

Glass cage

Try studying bugs up close, and you'll find they won't stay still. Look carefully under logs and stones, place the bugs gently in a jar, and put muslin over the top. (Set them free afterward.)

Night shift

Bugs that scuttle about by day aren't hard to find. But you need cunning to follow the night crawlers. Cut a grapefruit in half and scoop out the fleshy parts. Put the halves, face down, in your backyard overnight. Check in the morning to see which bugs dropped by for a snack.

A feasting woodlouse

Safe haven

If you want to look at a live bug, make a special observatory. Dig a hole, drop a yogurt cup inside it, and put in a piece of food – a chunk of cheese or some cookie crumbs. Balance a sheet of wood on four pebbles over the observatory to keep the bugs safe and dry.

Study your bugs carefully, then free them.

Swap your food now and then. Which kind attracts the most bugs?

Pooter power

Think of a vacuum cleaner without an engine. That's a pooter. It's a handy, harmless way to gently lift up small insects by using the power of human breath – but don't worry, you won't suck any into your mouth by mistake!

Cut two lengths of tubing – one 20 in (50 cm), and one half the size. Tie a piece of muslin around one end of the short tube with a rubber band.

Using tape, attach a piece of cardboard to the top of a jar, with two holes in the top for the tubes. Use modeling clay to wedge the tubes tight.

Bug science

Scientists have named about a million insect species, and some people believe that there may be millions more to be identified. Not all bugs are insects, however – only those with six legs and bodies divided into three parts – like this beetle.

Centipedes and millipedes are not insects because they have many legs. You can find them living under stones and logs.

Hold the long tube above the bug, give a short suck, and vacuum it into the pooter.

The muslin stops you from swallowing the bug.

⚠🦋Backyard Guests

IF YOU WANT TO GET TO KNOW the creatures that live in your backyard, why not make them feel so welcome they'll want to stay. By watching them going about their daily business, you can get a real feeling for how they live.

Caterpillar ranch

Observing butterflies is tricky, but caterpillars are much easier to keep an eye on. The best time to find caterpillars is in spring or early summer. Check out what species the caterpillar is and what it eats, then make a home for it in an empty tub with lots of the food it likes. The really fun part is watching them turn into butterflies and heading off into the wild.

Line the tub with paper towels and spray them lightly with water. Leave the caterpillars on the leaves or twigs that they live on and transfer everything into your tub. Feed them fresh leaves every day, keep the tub moist, and place muslin over the top.

Green is not a usual flower color. How many bees try it?

Are bees smart – do they go for the right one?

Caterpillar science

A butterfly lays caterpillar eggs on leaves that will come in handy later. When the caterpillar emerges it eats the leaves it is born on.

When the caterpillar is fully grown it turns into a pupa, which looks a bit like a dry piece of wood hanging off a leaf.

Honey, I trained the bees!

All summer long, bees drone from flower to flower gathering nectar. Use some fake nectar and encourage honeybees to visit your backyard. Cut three colored flower shapes out of cardboard. Place a bottle lid in the center of each one. Fill the blue flower lid with sugary water and the others with plain water. Leave them outside. When a bee has found some nectar, it flies back to its nest and does a waggle dance to tell the others where to get it. Do they go for the right flower?

How many bees are fooled by the plain water?

Inside the pupa a change takes place. The tissue of the caterpillar's body is broken down, and new organs and tissues develop. After a few weeks the butterfly is ready to struggle out. It looks bedraggled at first but after a few hours the wings dry and harden so that it can fly.

Snail expedition

Snails don't rush. But they are determined creatures, and they get where they want to in the end, leaving a slimy trail behind them. Collect some snails and paint a number on their shells. Put them back where you found them and keep track of their movements through the day. Which is the champion traveler? Where do they rest in your backyard?

Be careful not to get any paint on the snail itself, and wash your hands after handling them.

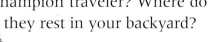

Night Life

BUGS HAVE ALL THE LUCK. Just as humans are getting tucked in bed, millions of insects are putting on their party clothes to go out for the night. Of course, it's just common sense. There are a lot fewer birds and people around to annoy them.

Bats sleep during the day by hanging upside down.

Moths love to sip sugary liquids with their long tongues.

Moth ball

Moths will think that you're holding a grand ball if you serve them this delicious cocktail one night. Paint some juice concentrate on a tree, shine a flashlight on it when it gets dark, and wait for your guests to show up. How many moths come to your feast?

Night noises

Except for snoring, night ought to be a time of peace and quiet. If only! Go into the backyard at dusk and keep very still. Depending on where you live, you may hear frogs croak, owls hoot, mosquitoes whine, crickets rub their knees, and, if you are lucky, the strangled bark of a fox. Keep a logbook of any nocturnal sounds that you can identify.

The hoot of an owl is a common sound at night.

Owls can turn their heads 270° each way!

Animal trackers

Wild animals are often shy so only appear at night. They skidaddle the moment they hear you coming. Here's a way to ensure that they leave their calling card. Lay a pile of sand on the ground, dampen it a little, and make sure it is smooth. You could put a bit of bait on it. Next morning check for any tracks.

Small, round paw prints such as these may be cats. A silver glistening trail is a snail or a slug.

Dew science

On clear, still nights when the air gets chilly, water vapor in the air becomes dew, which forms near the ground. Early in the morning, go outside and check out the dewy spider's webs with each strand glistening with moisture.

Night creatures

Unlike us humans, many animals sleep during the day and are active when it gets dark. Long ago, small mammals moved around in darkness to avoid being caught by hungry dinosaurs, and some have remained nocturnal to this day. This means that hunters such as foxes and owls have become active at night in order to catch them.

Glow by night

There are thousands of living things that glow at night like lightbulbs. The most common is the firefly, which is actually a beetle. It has a chemical in its body that makes it glow. Each species has its own code of signals, based on flashes, by which fireflies can "talk" to each other. Some scientists have measured the timing between flashes and so have learned to imitate the signals.

Smooth as silk

Amazingly enough, soft silk is produced from the hard cocoon of the silk moth. Each cocoon unravels into a thread of silk that can be over 0.6 miles (1 km) long in total.

Big Splash!

YOU CAN TAKE A BATH IN IT. You can brush your teeth in it. You can drink it. Even better, you can also use water to show off how much you know about science. Find out how amazing water can be and prepare to get wet!

Water whirl

If you hold a cup of water upside down it empties out, right? Not always. Fill a bucket of water about a quarter full and with a swift action swing it up and over your head in a full circle, over and over again. What happens to the water?

Don't be timid with the bucket, give it a really good swing.

Centrifugal science

The water stays in the bucket because it's held in by centrifugal force. When the bucket swings in a circle, the force drives the water against the bottom so hard that it overcomes the normal urge to flow out. This force also keeps you in your seat on a roller coaster.

Uphill flow

Did you know that it is possible to empty the liquid from one jar into another without pouring it? It's simple really. You'll need some plastic tubing. Then all you have to do is make the water flow uphill.

Fill a jar full of liquid, put a tube into it, and suck. Just before the liquid reaches your mouth, hold your thumb over the end.

Put the tube into the empty jar and hold the full jar up above the empty one. Let go with your thumb. What happens to the liquid?

The colors of the rainbow are always in the same order: red, orange, yellow, green, blue, indigo, and violet.

Making rainbows

You don't need rain to make a rainbow, you can create your very own in your backyard. Turn your back to the sun with your shadow straight ahead. Aim the hose so that the spray lands on the far side of the shadow. Do you see a perfect rainbow of color?

Syphon science

A syphon makes use of the fact that water can't help but flow from a high place to a low place. The pressure of the water in the high jar is strong enough to push water up the tube and over into the lower jar. Syphons are often used to clean fish tanks gently without disturbing the fish.

Make sure the end of the tube remains in the liquid.

Use your favorite drink in case it goes into your mouth by mistake.

The liquid flows from the full jar into the empty one, but to make this journey it has to climb uphill in part of the tube then down into the empty jar to fill it. How does this happen?

Rainbow science

Sunlight is made up of seven colors, which you normally don't see. As sunlight shines through droplets of water it bends a little. Each color bends at a slightly different angle and fans out to make a colorful arc of light called a rainbow.

Rain Check

THE GROUND IS COVERED IN PUDDLES, and the gutters are gurgling with water – perfect weather to study rain. Put on your raincoat, open your umbrella, and become a rain catcher. There are lots of things to discover about rainwater.

A little rain is no excuse not to take science outdoors.

Wet, wet, wet

In order to do rain experiments, you will first have to catch the rain. A rain gauge is the first step toward a working weather station (page 28). When you have trapped some rain, test it to see how acidic it is using this acid test.

To make a rain gauge, take a bucket out into the yard and place it in an open space. Stand a stick down the side of the bucket. Check every day for rain, and when you have logged it on your weather chart tip it into a jar to use for your acid rain test. Keep a record every day of the rainfall in your backyard.

Acid science

Pollution from cars and chimneys does funny things to rain. The fumes dissolve in it and turn the rain slightly acid. Acid rain eats away soft stone on many buildings, and if it's very strong it can kill trees too.

Record the rainfall every day for a month, then compare each day.

Litmus paper darkens slightly in tap water.

Compare the litmus in the rainwater with the tap water and very acidic vinegar.

Litmus will go very pink in the acidic vinegar.

Here's a way to test the kind of rain that's coming down on you. Fill three jars – one with tap water, one with rainwater, and one with vinegar. Insert a piece of litmus paper into each one. The pinker your litmus paper, the more acidic the rain is.

Care for a sip?
You wouldn't gulp water from a muddy puddle (unless you were dying of thirst) because you wouldn't know if it was OK to drink. But tap water starts out as rain on the ground. So how does it end up clean to drink? The answer is a water filter. This basic filter works in the same way as the ones that give you clean tap water.

On an island in Hawaii it rains about 350 days per year!

Carefully pour the puddle water into the flowerpot. The gravel traps the large pieces of dirt floating in the water, the sand catches small pieces, and the blotting paper traps the finest specks of dirt. Compare the water seeping out of the bottom to the puddle water. Don't drink it, however. It may be clearer but it's not yet pure.

Make sure that the blotting paper covers the whole of the bottom of the flowerpot.

Line the bottom of a flowerpot with blotting paper. Fill the pot half full with fine sand and then fill it to the top with gravel. Place the flowerpot onto a jar. Take some dirty rainwater from a puddle and stir it.

Find some really dirty puddle water to filter.

Rain science

So how does rainwater get so clean by the time it runs out of our faucets? Here's how.

The rainwater makes its way into a reservoir and is then sucked into pipes by huge pumps. Large objects, such as twigs, are removed at this point.

Two chemicals are added to the water. They make specks of dirt cling together so that they sink.

The water flows into a sedimentation tank where the dirt forms a sludge at the bottom. The sludge is then removed.

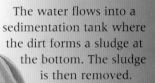

Now the water is filtered, through sand and gravel, just like your water filter to get rid of the last little bits of dirt. And it's ready to drink.

27

Weather Report

HOW DO THEY DO IT? Day after day TV weather forecasters look into the camera and tell us what tomorrow's weather will be like. But how can they be so sure? Or are they just guessing? Make your own weather station and keep a chart to monitor the weather.

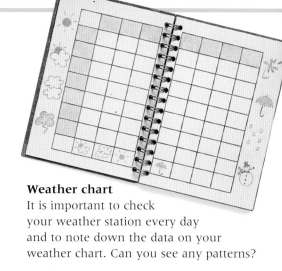

Weather chart
It is important to check your weather station every day and to note down the data on your weather chart. Can you see any patterns?

The instruments

The main pieces of equipment that you will need are a barometer to measure air pressure, a thermometer to measure temperature, a wind machine to measure wind direction and speed, and a rain gauge (see page 26) to measure the amount of rainfall.

If the pointer falls then the pressure is falling – bad weather on the way.

No weather station is complete without a thermometer. Record the temperature daily on your weather chart.

A barometer measures air pressure – the weight of air that presses down on the ground. The air pressure falls if a storm is near, and rises when fine weather is approaching. Here's how to make your own. Cut off a balloon's neck with a pair of scissors and stretch the rest over a jar. Fasten the sides down with tape. Fasten two straws together and tape one end to the center of the balloon. Stand a ruler up and measure the movement of the marker every day.

Wind machine

Weather forecasters use a wind vane to tell them the direction the wind is coming from, and an anemometer to tell them how hard it's blowing. Here's how to build the two machines in one.

On a square piece of plastic, draw an arc of 90°. Mark from 0° to 90° with a protractor at 10° intervals. Cut out a pointer and a tail and attach one at either end of a 23.5 in (60 cm) piece of bamboo.

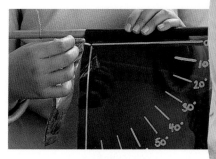

Attach the square piece of plastic to the bamboo with tape, as shown. Take a long piece of aluminum foil and tape it to one end of a toothpick. Pierce the plastic square at the top and slide the toothpick through the hole so that the foil strip can swing freely. Tie a thick piece of wire around the center of the bamboo leaving a long prong below it. Insert the wire prong into a long piece of bamboo.

What's blowing?

Weather comes with the wind, so if the wind changes it's usually a sign that something is brewing. Weather forecasters use a vane to show them which direction the wind is coming from. To measure wind speed, note the degree the swinging strip reaches. 90° means no wind, more than 50° means stay indoors!

The swinging foil shows the wind speed.

The wire prong should allow the vane to swing around freely in the wind.

Use a compass to mark north, south, east, and west on a flowerpot base and note the wind direction.

Forecasting

So how do we predict the weather? There are over 10,000 weather stations all over the world, which send information to forecasting centers. Many stations send up balloons with instruments attached – the drift measures wind speed and direction, and the instruments hold other information. They rise to about 12-19 miles (20-30 km) then they burst dropping instruments, which fall by parachute.

Weather satellites orbit the Earth and show pictures of the weather conditions (see below.) With all this daily information, no wonder forecasters have a good idea of tomorrow's weather.

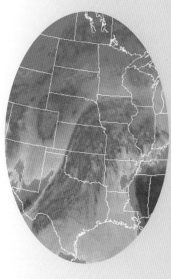

Shadow Catching

ON A FRESH MORNING, as the sunlight plays among the trees, shadows dapple the ground wherever you look. It's perfect weather for proving that the Sun is a clock and also that the Earth is moving.

Shadow time

It's time to prove that we can tell the time by using the Sun. Stand a stick in a flowerpot in a sunny area. Every hour mark where the stick's shadow falls using a small flowerpot with the time written on it. The next day the shadows fall at the same time. The sun measures time very well – as long as we know how to read it.

Ray ban
Sunlight travels in straight lines called "rays." When rays hit something solid they get blocked. On the far side of the tree where sunlight can't reach, a patch of "no rays" forms – a shadow.

Shadow science

The Earth spins around once every 24 hours, which means that at any time half the Earth faces the Sun and enjoys daylight (day) and half is in shadow (night). As the Sun seems to move from east to west the shadows it casts appear to move too. But actually it's us that moves, not the Sun.

By using these shadows, you will find you have a timepiece!

When did we learn to tell the time?

It took thousands of years to figure out that the Earth did a twirl in 24 hours. The Babylonians were the first to work it out 4,000 years ago by watching the Sun travel across the sky. They made the first sundials – a sundial has a pointer called a gnomon, and the gnomon's shadow shows the time on a flat dial marked in hours.

The gnomon's shadow points to the time.

Galloping shadows

Shadows shrink and grow throughout the day. They are at their biggest in the morning and again in the evening. Prove this by standing in exactly the same spot several times during the day.
Each time, get a friend to mark the tip of your shadow with a stick. When is your shadow the longest, or shortest?

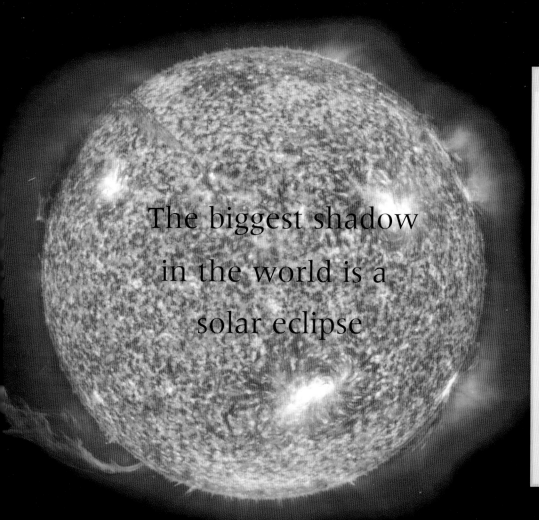

The biggest shadow
in the world is a
solar eclipse

The ultimate shadow

The biggest shadow you can ever hope to see is the shadow of the Moon as it falls across the surface of the Earth. This is an eclipse of the Sun. From the ground it looks like the Sun is being eaten away by the Moon until it is completely hidden.

The Sun is hidden by the Moon.

An eclipse forms when the Sun, Earth, and Moon line up so that the Moon lies between us and the Sun. Then the shadow of the Moon sweeps over the Earth. If the eclipse is total, it turns day into night for a few minutes. If you were an astronaut hanging around out in space, this is what you would see. A big shadow where the Moon partly hides the Sun (a partial eclipse) and a smaller, darker shadow where it blocks all of the Sun (total eclipse).

The light from the Sun travels toward the Earth as if on a normal sunny day.

The Moon moves between the Sun and the Earth.

The Moon's shadow causes a total eclipse on one part of the Earth.

⚠ Soil Science

IT MAKES YOU DIRTY. It gets you mucky. And a single spoonful of it would taste disgusting. Yet without it we would all starve. "It" is soil – the stuff from which our vegetables, our fruit, and even our meat (in a roundabout way) comes. But what exactly is soil?

Crawling under your feet

Soil is crawling with thousands of creatures. Animals, such as moles and worms, appear above ground every so often and are large enough to spot. Here's how to meet some of the tiny creatures you rarely see. Take handfuls of soil from different parts of your backyard.

A small patch of soil holds millions of worms, insects, grubs, and fungi.

Rest a funnel in a jar. Put a handful of soil in a sieve and put it in the funnel. Bend a lamp close over the soil and leave it for about half an hour. The little creatures in the soil are not used to light and will burrow away from it until they drop out of the funnel into the jar. Tip the creatures into a saucer and, using a magnifying glass, study them close up. (Do not leave them under the light for too long – they might overheat.)

How many different types of animals appear in your jar?

Make a record of the ones you find. Try to identify them later.

Something rotten

Nature doesn't waste a thing.
As soon as a plant or animal dies
it rots, or decays. Slice a red pepper,
or any other fruit or vegetable, in
half. Place it on a dish, and day by
day watch what takes place. What
does it look like after two weeks?

Rotten science

The living organisms in the soil are nature's
recyclers. They include bacteria, fungi, and
various animals. Their job is to break
down dead organic material (plants
and animals) and let the nutrients
they contain back into the soil so
that other plants grow healthily.
Worms are very good recyclers –
find out how by turning the page.

What's in it?

Soil is a mixture of all sorts of things. We know
that it contains living organisms and decaying
plants and animals, but what else is there?
Gather soil samples from your backyard and
put them into jars. Add water so that the jars
are nearly full. Shake well then let them stand.

Rotten plants and animals (organic matter)
float at the top of the water, and rocks and
minerals sink. Rock fragments will sink first,
sandy pieces will settle as the next layer. Fine
clay sinks slowly and sits on the sand.

Soil from different
areas will contain
varying amounts
of minerals and
organic matter.

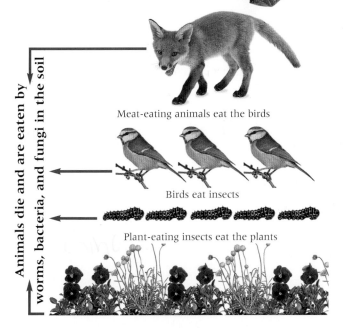

Animals die and are eaten by
worms, bacteria, and fungi in the soil

Meat-eating animals eat the birds

Birds eat insects

Plant-eating insects eat the plants

Say hello to dinner

Every plant and animal in the world is
dinner for something else. Even human
beings, after they die and are buried, end up
as meals for worms and bacteria. The route
from one stomach to the next is called a
food chain. There are many kinds of food
chains. Take a look at the simple one above.

⚠ Worm Farm

EVERYBODY LOVES WORMS. Gardeners like them because they make gardens healthy. Birds like them as a tasty meal. And once you understand what an amazing job they do, you'll start to enjoy them too.

Home from home

A worm farm gives us the chance to find out what happens underground. Fill a bowl with alternate layers of soil and sand. Put some leaves and veggies on the top. Add water to make the soil damp and let some worms make themselves at home.

Charmed, I'm sure
Worm charming is a great way to watch worms. Pretend to be a shower of rain by jumping up and down. The worms will come to the surface to enjoy the drops.

Fallen leaves   Soil   Fine sand

Keep the worm farm somewhere cool and dark.

Heads or tails?

One way not to tell the head of a worm from the tail is by listening to which end snores. It's actually very hard to tell. Luckily there's a simple way to find out. Place a worm in a dish and touch one end very gently. The worm shrinks back. Now touch the other end; it shrinks back too but the end that shrinks the quickest is the tail.

Worms have sensitive tails that pull back rapidly if touched. This is an escape reaction in case a bird tries to grab on before they can hide.

The saddle – the thick part that carries the eggs.

Worm walk

Look closely at an earthworm. You will notice that it is divided into segments – muscles. The worm also has a long muscle running right through its body. To move, the worm contracts the segments and stretches its body muscle forward. Tiny bristles help it grip the soil. Next the worm contracts its long muscle and draws up the rest of the body behind the front section so moving forward.

Worm science

Earthworms are vital to the soil. On the surface they eat decaying plants and animals and then, as they move through the soil, the food passes through the worm and is deposited behind it in the tunnels it digs. This mixes the soil up and distributes the nutrients from above. The tunnels also let the soil breathe and help rainwater to drain away.

Without earthworms, the soil would become hard and airless.

Check every day, and you'll soon see tunnels as worms eat through the soil. The layers of soil will start to mix, and leaves will be pulled into the tunnels. After the project, put the worms back where you found them.

Worm secrets

• Worms have no bones. They are bendable and squishy and have skin you can see through.

• There are over 1,800 species of earthworms in the world.

• One Australian species of earthworm can grow as long as 11 ft (3.3 m). That's the size of two humans lying lengthwise.

⚠ On Tap

FOR ANIMALS, A POND in the garden is like us having faucets in the bathroom. It means a regular supply of water to drink and water to have a bath in. Even a minipond is a magnet for wildlife. All you need is a quiet corner of your backyard that gets a little sun.

If you spot a creature lurking in the pondweed, scoop it gently into a jar of water (return it carefully when you have finished studying it).

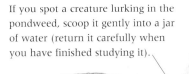

⚠ Minipond

To make your own minipond you will need some real pond water. Go to a pond near you and, with an adult, collect some water in a bowl. Dig a hole in your yard and lower the bowl until the rim is level with the ground. Add some pondweed (from a local nursery) and some stones and pebbles so that the water animals have somewhere to hide.

Pond science

Pond water is already full of all sorts of goodies that your visitors will like, but tap water will do just as well. Plants are essential in a pond as they supply oxygen and keep the water fresh. Keep the pond filled up in hot weather.

Feel the tension

Here is an experiment to show that insects can walk on water. Simply fill a glass with water and drop a matchstick onto it. Surface tension lets the match rest on top of the surface. It doesn't even get wet!

Surface science

Now and then you may see water spiders skittering across your pond. They are so light that they can sit on water without sinking into it. They make use of a special force called surface tension. It pulls the surface of water together so much that it forms a stretchy skin. Surface tension is why raindrops are round and why water spiders glide about without getting wet. Sadly, it's not strong enough to hold up humans.

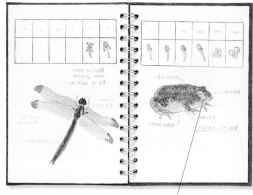

Draw the animals in as much detail as you can.

Pond logbook

Keep a pond logbook. As the days go by, all kinds of small insects will visit. Some, like damselflies, may even lay their eggs in it. Snails and frogs may come to it, and birds will drink from it.

Dragonflies, like minihelicopters, can hover, dart backward, make 90° turns, and come to an instant stop.

Frogs can breathe through their skin as well as their nostrils.

Flying dragons

Look out for dragonflies that lay their eggs in ponds, and watch them fly at lightning speed – a dragonfly's wings flap about 20 times a second.

Large clumps of frogspawn float near the surface and are easy to find.

Frog march

Here's something to watch out for in ponds. In spring, frogs lay huge amounts of frogspawn. Look in your pond, or a local pond, for the jellylike eggs. Watch them, and within two or three weeks the eggs will turn into tadpoles and then into frogs. If you are lucky enough to find some eggs, keep a log of their growth.

Look up it. Try to guess how tall and how old it is. Then read on and see how accurate you were!

Tree of Life

THEY ARE ALL AROUND US and stretch high above us. But ask a simple question about trees, like how old they are, and people are stumped! Here's how to measure a tree's size and figure out how old it is.

How tall?

Measuring a tree is a little harder than measuring a human. You can't just pick it up and measure it against a wall. It is, however, much easier than you imagine. All you need is a stick, a long piece of string, a steady hand, and a friend.

Position a friend at the bottom of the tree. Stand a good distance back and hold a stick out straight in front of you. Make your thumb level with the bottom of the tree and the top of the stick level with the crown.

Happy birthday to yew!

You can roughly work out the age of a tree by measuring around the trunk, about 60 in (150 cm) above the ground. Divide the answer by 1 in (2.5 cm) to find the approximate age. Some trees are not suitable experiments – for example, yew and redwood.

Sap alert

Trees have sap inside that runs all the way up to the top. Trees like pines have a special, sticky sap. It flows out of cuts in order to keep off bugs and other animals while the wound heals and new bark grows over it.

How big?

The California redwoods are the tallest trees in the world. Their trunks can grow up to 25 ft (7.5 m) wide. From base to towering top they can reach a staggering 278 ft (85 m).

Growing old

Bristlecone pines in California are the oldest trees in the world. Some have been around for over 4,000 years – they were in their prime when the Pharaohs ruled Egypt. Imagine what they could tell us if they had memories.

Try to track down the tallest tree in your neighborhood.

The most accurate way to tell a tree's age is to count rings. A tree adds one ring each year.

There's only one way to find the age of a tree that's 100% accurate – unfortunately it involves chopping it down!

Keeping your thumb very still, swivel the stick sideways until it is level with the ground. Ask your friend to walk away from the tree and stand at the end of the stick. Go over and give them an end of string. Run the string back to the base of the tree, measure it, and there you have it – the height.

Move it!

GARDENING CAN BE BACK-BREAKING work. But thanks to levers you have no excuse because they make lots of tiring jobs so much easier. They change a little effort from you into enough power to haul a great big, heavy load.

What a drag!

When you've been gardening and you have a full sack of garbage, you'll find it pretty hard to lift. You may just be able to drag it across the yard, but don't overdo it. Help is at hand.

Think about how the wheelbarrow works to help you move this load.

Levers make

light work of some

really heavy

backyard tasks

Now put the load into a wheelbarrow and trundle it to the other end of the garden. Easier? How long does it take you to get it across now? The wheelbarrow is one of the most useful garden levers. It's a machine that seems to give you extra strength. That's what levers are all about – turning you into a superkid.

Wheelbarrow races

The trick with a lever is to get exactly the right balance between the fulcrum, load, and effort to make the load lightest. Have a wheelbarrow race with your friends and find out where to put your "load" so that you can move fastest.

Try putting your friend near to the handle end of the wheelbarrow. The load (your friend) is nearer the effort (you) so you will find that she is difficult to lift – it's quite a struggle.

Now place her at the other end – over the fulcrum. Now that the fulcrum is taking most of her weight, the wheelbarrow is easier to push. You'll probably win the race.

Lever power

You are pedaling at full speed down a hill, and a cat strays in front of you. You slam on the brakes and stop instantly. Wow – talk about finger power! It's all due to the levers that sit between your fingers and the wheels. (The brake handle is a lever, and both brake arms are levers too.) They multiply your strength until it can stop your weight, the bike's weight, and the speed of both in the space of just a few yards.

Everyday levers

Did you know that parts of your body are levers too? Take your foot. When you take a step, the ball of your foot becomes the fulcrum, the load is your body weight, and the effort that moves is in all your leg muscles. Try to think of other levers that you use every day. From little levers – nail clippers and nutcrackers – to larger levers – garden shears and scales – to massive levers like huge diggers.

How on earth can you move such a heavy object more easily?

Lever science

Here comes the science part. All levers move up and down around a point called a "fulcrum." With it, the lever raises and lowers the "load." The force that does all the hard work of shifting the load is the "effort." And that, in a nutshell, is levers. On the wheelbarrow, the wheel acts as the fulcrum. The load is the sack, and your grip on the handles is the effort. The wheelbarrow is a good lever so makes light work of a job.

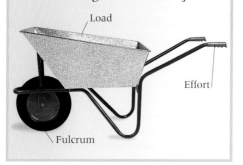
Load
Effort
Fulcrum

Fast Brains

DID YOU KNOW THAT YOUR BRAIN is lightning quick? It can sense and react to something faster than you can say "ouch." Test yourself to find out how speedy it is.

Mark the ground with a rope and stand with your arms out – easy!

Now lift a foot. This halves the balance information that the feet send to the brain. Are you still steady?

Ask a friend to blindfold you. Now your eyes can't tell your brain where the ground is. You'll be wobbling hard!

Wobble test

Toddlers fall over all the time. Why don't you? Because as you grow up, your brain learns what to do if the ground slopes suddenly – and you develop a sense of balance. Try this trick if you've forgotten what it's like to wobble like a toddler.

How long can you stay upright on one foot?

Finally hold your arms by your sides – arms help you balance. Now you'll find it pretty hard to stand at all. Most people fall over at this point!

42

Eye ball

Sometimes your hands are so quick they seem to have a mind of their own – like when they catch a flying ball. Throw a ball into the air and catch it – fairly easy. Now do it with your eyes closed – bonk!

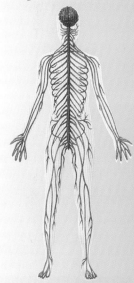

Body science

So why does your body know how to remain steady and upright all the time (well, almost all the time)? Or how do you catch a ball when it is thrown to you?

Well, your brain has an image of your body and knows what position your arms, legs, trunk, and head must be in to remain upright. Senses in parts of the body, such as in the eyes, muscles, ears, and skin send high-speed messages to the brain through nerve branches.

Why is it hard to catch with eyes shut? Because your brain has no idea where your hands are supposed to be.

Quick reaction

Test the speed of your brain's reactions with this simple game. Tie four colored pieces of tape around a stick and ask a friend to hold it just above your hand. Get him to drop it without warning while you snap your fingers shut as quickly as possible to catch it. What color did you grab near? The nearer your finger was to the bottom, the faster your brain worked. Can you train your brain to speed up by practicing?

If any of these senses are taken away, your brain doesn't get all the information it needs, and your body will not behave correctly. In the wobble test, your brain only has one leg on the ground so it uses your arms and eyes to balance. Your eyes are then subtracted and lastly your arms. Now your brain has too little information to keep you upright. In the ball test, the most vital sense – the eyes – is taken away.

Signals are flashed back and forth to your brain at up to 330 ft (100 m) per second

Heartbeat

YOUR HEART IS THE STRONGEST thing in your whole body. It pumps all day and all night for a lifetime without stopping. Put your heart and lungs to the test and find out how strong your body is.

Heart work

When your heart beats, it sends a wave of blood through your body – this is called a pulse. If you are active, the pulse beats faster and your lungs work harder so you breathe faster too. Measure your heartrate and breaths after exercise to see out how much more work they do.

Before you exercise, time with a stopwatch how often you breathe in one minute. Next count your pulse rate for a minute. Find your pulse by holding your forefinger and middle finger on your wrist. The average for a 10-year-old is 80 beats per minute.

Now go and do some vigorous exercise.

Right after exercise, check your breathing rate. Count how many breathes your lungs take in a minute. How many more breathes do your lungs need now compared to before?

Time a minute while you count your pulse. How much faster is it? Now time how long your breathing and pulse rates take to return to normal. The quicker they recover, the fitter you are.

The heart of the matter

You know how many times your heart beats per minute, but have you ever thought about how hard it works to pump blood all around your body? Fill one bowl with water and place an empty one next to it. Use a half-pint (150 ml) sized beaker to bale water 80 times in a minute from the full bowl to the empty one. Ask a friend to time you. How tired is your arm?

Every minute, your heart pumps this much blood.

Blood science

The heart has a muscle that never gets tired. It can pump away for a whole lifetime without ever needing a vacation. It also pumps very hard – over 14,000 quarts a day. When the body is active it needs more oxygen, which is absorbed through the lungs and carried in the blood. Then the heart must beat even faster to get blood around the body.

Pump power

As a rule of thumb, bigger animals have slower heartbeats than smaller ones. For example, adult humans have slower rates than children and babies. This huge elephant has a heart that dawdles along at about 25 to 30 beats per minute.

The tiny mouse's heart races at about 500 beats per minute.

Did you know?

If the inner surfaces of your lungs were laid out flat, they would cover an area more than two-thirds the size of a tennis court!

After Dark

IF SOMEONE TOLD YOU THAT people can hardly see a thing by daylight, you would think they were crazy. But it's true. By day we can only see one star in the universe, the Sun, but by night we can see zillions. So if you really want to find out more about the universe, stay up late.

Moon science

As the Moon circles the Earth it changes shape day by day. Not a clever trick, just the way the Moon sails in and out of the shadow of the Earth while it orbits us. The changing shapes are called the "phases" of the Moon.

Full Moon

Waning Gibbous

Waxing Gibbous

Last Quarter

First Quarter

Waning Crescent

New Moon
(not visible from Earth)

Waxing Crescent

Ocean of Storms

Moon watch

The best way to study the Moon is flat on your back looking through a pair of binoculars on a clear night. Track the changing shapes of the Moon (phases) and fill in this Moon chart of a lunar month.

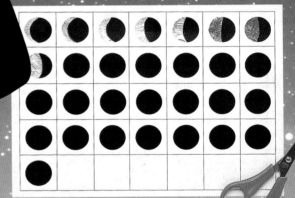

Draw up a chart with seven columns and five rows. Draw 29 black circles in each box. Every night, cut the Moon's shape out of aluminum foil and stick it onto a black circle. How long until the Moon looks like it did in the first box again? (This is because it has completed one orbit of the Earth.)

Sea of Rains

Appenine Mountains

Sea of Serenity

Copernicus
Crater

Sea of Vapors

Sea of Tranquility

Ptolomaeus
Crater

Sea of Clouds

Tycho
Crater

Moonscapes
The Moon is the nearest thing in
the sky. On a clear night you can see
surprising details. The best time to
study the Moon is when it's growing
from a crescent shape to a full circle –
that's when it is visible at the right
time of night. The seas are plains
of dark lava (people once thought
they held water). At full Moon
watch for the bright rays that
extend from the crater Tycho.

Did you know?
Did you know that on
Earth we only ever see
one side of the Moon?
The only humans who
have ever seen the
other side are
astronauts who have
flown around it.

Sky racers
When meteors enter
Earth's atmosphere they
heat up and burn. This
makes them appear to
streak across the sky
at night. We call these
"shooting stars." Look
out for them low
on the horizon.

Night sight
It takes about half an
hour for eyes to adjust to
the dark in order to see
faint stars. So if you want
to make notes or study
a star map, you'll need a
night light. Cover the lens
of a flashlight with red
cellophane and tape
it down tightly. The red
glow is so dim that it
won't wipe out your
night vision.

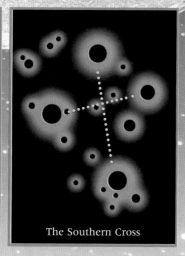

Polaris
(The North
Star)

The Plow

The Southern Cross

Compass stars
If you are in the
Northern Hemisphere,
face north using a
compass, then look up
slowly, and you will see
the North Star. If you
are in the Southern
Hemisphere, aim the
compass south to find
the Southern Cross.

Index

Acknowledgments

Chris Maynard has written about 55 children's books. He won the Rhone-Poulenc Science Junior Book of the Year in 1996 (*The World of Weather*) and his *Informania Sharks* was runner up for the TES Senior Information Book Award in 1998. Recently, he has discovered the joys of writing websites too.

Dorling Kindersley would like to thank the following people for their help in the production of this book: Janet Allis for additional design help, Andy Crawford for additional photography, Tracey Simmonds for photography assistance, Lara Tankel Holtz for the loan of her garden, Adrian Hall Garden Centres for the equipment, and the parents of the budding scientists for their patience.

The publisher would like to thank the following for their kind permission to reproduce their images:
Position key: c=center; b=bottom; l=left; r=right; t=top.
Britstock-ifa: Number Three Co 10c. **Corbis UK Ltd**: Roger Garwood & Trish Ainslie 29cr. **Robert Harding Picture Library**: Nedra Westwater 30BL. **N.A.S.A.**: 29br. **N.H.P.A.**: 13CR; E A Janes 11cr; Stephen Dalton 21br, 22tr. **Powerstock Photolibrary / Zefa**: 3R. **Science Photo Library**: 9TR; Andrew Syred 35cr; Claude Nuridsany and Maria Perennous 37C(above); Dr Fred Espenak 31CR(above); John Sanford 46-47, 47t; Keith Kent 23crb. **gettyone stone**: 8TR, 17CR; Darrell Gulin Endpapers; J F Causse 10tr; J. F. Causse 30TR; Michael Orton 2C; Oliver Strewe 26c. **Telegraph Colour Library**: John Wilkes 27tr; Tony Bennett 23cb. **Woodfall Wild Images**: 13BR.